Uncharted

Mitali Parewa

Uncharted © 2023 Mitali Parewa

All rights reserved.

No part of this publication may be reproduced, stored in a retrieval system, or transmitted, in any form or by any means, electronic, mechanical, photocopying, recording or otherwise, without the prior written permission of the presenters.

Mitali Parewa asserts the moral right to be identified as the author of this work.

Presentation by *BookLeaf Publishing*

Web: www.bookleafpub.com

E-mail: info@bookleafpub.com

ISBN: 9789358738124

First edition 2023

To all my readers,

*Your mere existence on this planet itself is a
poem.*

PREFACE

In the realm of modernity, where the relentless pursuit of success often eclipses our most vital relationship—with ourselves—emerges a voice, unexpected yet profound.

The poems contained within these pages are not merely words; they are echoes of vulnerability and resilience, reflections of solitude and connection, and an invitation to pause and contemplate the importance of self-awareness amidst life's ceaseless demands.

This book serves as a compilation of the myriad thoughts that cross our minds each day – reflections on the experiences we undergo, the weariness that permeates our long and draining days, the sincere gratitude evoked by moments spent gazing at someone we hold dear, and the countless reflections that emerge every time we meet our own gaze in the mirror.

I trust that as you read this, you'll experience a profound sense of comfort and a connection not only to everyone around you but also to your surroundings, to our shared planet, and, most importantly, to the core of who you are.

Welcome to a poetry book that bridges the gap between the analytical and the artistic, the pragmatic and the profound—a book that invites you to embrace the beauty of love in each and every form, one verse at a time.

Much Love,
Mitali

TABLE OF CONTENTS

In the dance of pages, I've choreographed four graceful sections. Find the rhythm that resonates with you and let the poetry unfold in its elegant symphony.

METAPHYSICAL MIRROR

INWARD ILLUMINATION

NATURE'S NOVELTIES

ENCHANTED ECHOES

METAPHYSICAL MIRROR

Welcome to the philosophical exploration of existence through the eloquence of poetry. Within these verses, the enigma of existence unfolds, weaving inquiries into the fabric of being and the profound mysteries of life. Join this contemplative journey as each line unravels the threads of thought, inviting readers to ponder the timeless questions that echo through the corridors of human existence.

3 am Grief

How come we don't talk enough
About the 3 am grief
When it feels like
The world is falling apart
Right in front of you
And you can't stand up straight on your own two
feet
When it feels like
The silence of the night
Is going to eat you alive from the inside
And you hear your own screams all night
Do tears roll down your cheeks too
Like a berserk waterfall
How come we don't talk enough
About the grief that comes only during
The nighttime
Does it haunt you too?

Am I Content?

Don't quite know what this feeling is,
Am I content
Because I am finally home?
Or
Is it because I am not home anymore?

 -Journey of a person who moved
cities/countries

Morally grey

How does it feel
To be morally grey
To be free of living in cages
To be free of conforming
To be free of proving yourself
Tell me.
Is it a relief?
Or
Just another war at bay?

Open wound

It's like an open wound
Being a one-sided lover
No matter how much you try
To hide the pain
To cover up the bruises
All it takes is
One little smile and those glittery eyes
One little glimpse from the side of their eye
And you are right back
To where you started
At square one
On your knees
Again

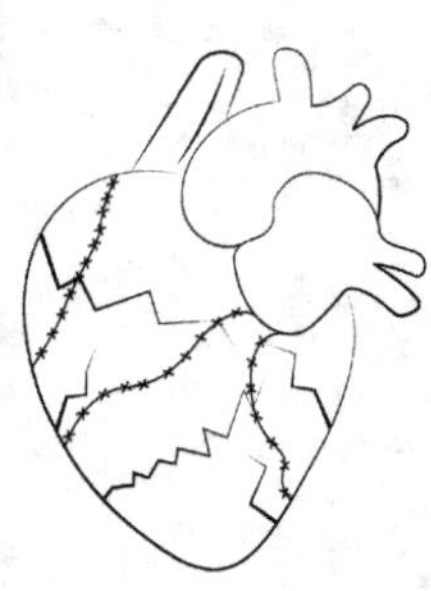

Blessing or curse?

It's not that I want to cease to exist
I just want to exist
Without being anything to anyone for a while
Just for a little while
I might be a little selfish
You might find it vain

I just want to be everything to me
For a few miles

Don't know if it's a blessing or a curse
My own life doesn't feel like my own at times
I have too many people relying on me
I have too many people waiting for me
Too much love
And
Too many expectations

Armour

Spent too much time tending to my armour
I forgot to tend to my wounds
Spent too much time shining it
I forgot to wipe the blood off my scars
Spent too much time strengthening it
I forgot to let go of the pain
Now I have a strong armor
To protect me from external harm
But I think
I am bleeding from the inside

Remember

Finally choosing yourself
After choosing others throughout your life
Might feel a lot like
Betraying yourself at that time
Now
Read it again
And
Let it sink in

Behind the camera

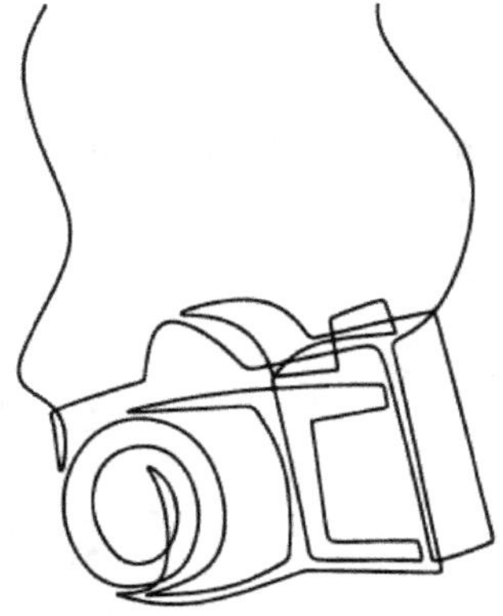

I wonder which one of us
Are happier?

The ones in front of all the cameras
Or
The ones behind these closed curtains

The ones living in the spotlight
Or
The ones walking past the streetlights

The lights are different
When you see them
Through your eyes
They are different
When you see them

Through your camera lens

So,
Tell me
Do the cameras help you hide your truth
Or
Do they expose it?

Secrets

I live in a constant fear of
Keeping my secrets safe
So that they don't get used against me
Also
I live in a constant fear of
Keeping my secrets safe
Worrying nobody will ever get to know
The real me.

A Fair Bargain

We often see things impartially
Concluding that
We have to pay such a heavy tax in love
We either end up losing the person
Or
We end up losing ourselves
Towards the end
Seeing it objectively one can conclude that
Pain
Loss
Suffering
Are not punishments
These are just the prices we pay
In exchange
For gaining the wonderful ability
To love

To our heart's content
Without any limits
And
More often than not
The fate that we get
Is not given to us by the universe
Instead, it is chosen by us
When we choose our lovers

Types

You will meet 2 types of people in life
The ones who will appreciate you more
The minute you take your clothes off
And
The ones who will appreciate you more
The minute you take your mask off

Let's try to stick with the latter ones, shall we?

Longing

I have a longing
For a place, I have never been to,
But
I am sure it is my home
I have a longing
For these people that I have never met,
But
I am sure they are my people
I have a longing
For a guy I have never seen before,
But
I love him with all of my heart

I have a longing
For a life
I have never seen

But
I am sure I have lived before

And it is growing
With every passing day
With every passing minute
And I don't know quite what to say
Except that
I am ready
I am finally ready to go home.

Possibilities

So, tell me.
Which one is crazier?
To believe in the impossible
Or
To believe that it is impossible
If ever given a chance
Which one would you choose
To believe in the impossibilities
Or
To be free of them
After all, liberation is not a sin
And neither is delusion.

Lenses

We all see the world through different lenses
Some of us wear our rose lenses
Which makes everything around us cheerful and
happy

Some of us just can't get rid of the tinted ones
That were forced upon us
Which makes everything around us gloomy and
empty

While the rest of us willingly choose the grey
ones
Not wanting to choose either of the extremes

I just hope every once in a while
We can take the burden off of each other

By exchanging our lenses
By giving each other
The space and comfort
To take them off for a while
Let it be known what a neutral palette looks like
It might not do or mean much at the moment
But need I remind you
It takes just a little crack in the surface
For the light to enter
And
Illuminate your world all over again.

Romeo & Juliet

I like Romeo and Juliet
Not just because it's tragically beautiful
But because it is a reflection of how we are
As humans on this planet
Living this life
Smiling through the pain
Fighting for our peace
Pushing through the hardships
And most importantly loving endlessly
Making each and every moment count
And making this existence
Tragically beautiful.

Alternatives

Tell me, my love
How many times have you turned up the volume
To let the music drown you
So that you don't drown yourself in pain

How many times have you picked up your pen
So that you don't pick up the knife
How many times have you decided to hang
around people
So that you don't hang by a noose

Crossroads

I remember
Being there
On the crossroads
On one side was my mind waiting
To take over
And
On the other was my love
Wanting to start over
All that love
That was growing inside of me
Taking over my each breath
All that love that I have for him
Knowing that choosing the former will make me
leave my love behind
Will put a spin on my mind
Will change me
From inside
Might make me less kind
And there will come a time
When there will be indifference
And
Our thoughts won't intertwine
My atoms will be different from his atoms
But in the end,
they will be mine
I will lose a part of me

I might be a little less me
But
I might just discover
The secret ingredient
And
I might end up finding the real key.

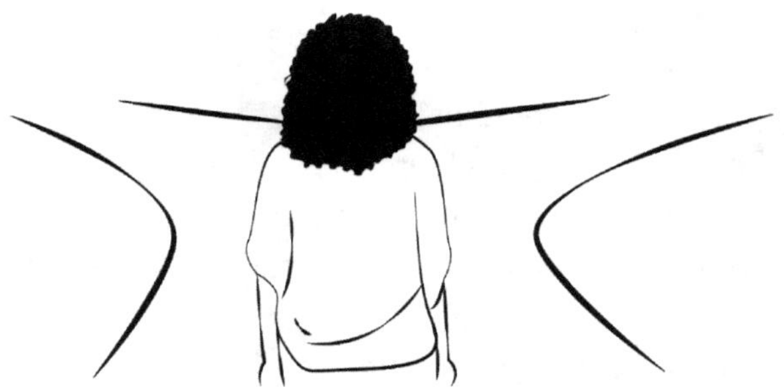

Home

If I ask you
Where is that one place, you go to
When you feel too overwhelmed with this world
And with your existence
How long would it take you to mention your
own name?
When will it be when you will finally go back
home
To yourself?

Happy Endings

I don't believe in happy endings
I do however believe in happy journeys

You see a chapter that ends
It is always
A misery for either one
Like a sage for you to burn

However,
During your journey
There will always be spaces in time
Like glitters in wine

There will be time
Full of bliss
And
Every moment will shine

Each and every moment spent together
Will feel heavenly
You will be all glee
And
Everyone involved will feel heavenly
Your heart won't ache
It won't make you race
There will just be smiles throughout

In every moment and state
It will feel like pure bliss
And every second will feel like an eternity
And that's how you will know
This journey was worth every single misery.

Consistency

The crushing pain you feel
When you feel like you are being a burden
But you can't help it
Can you?
You need them constantly
You need constant reassurance
You need constant care
You need constant love
You need constant comfort
But you feel like you are asking for too much
Too much of their effort
Too much of their time
Guess what
People who love you want to be there
They willingly choose
They choose you
They choose to stay by your side
They choose to fight your battles with you

And it is not a burden
For the ones who love you
It is a privilege
To love you
You are not asking for too much
Just asking the wrong ones maybe?

INWARD ILLUMINATIONS

28

Embark on a journey of introspection and empowerment within the pages of this section. Here, verses serve as mirrors reflecting the nuanced facets of the self, echoing the resilience and strength that lie within. Let these words be a source of inspiration, guiding you towards the empowerment that blossoms when one embraces the depths of self-awareness and the transformative power of inner strength.

A little something

I know how you are so outgoing yet so closed
off
Maybe you just want someone to peel those
layers off,

I know how you are so bold yet a little shy
Maybe you just want someone to hold your hand
and make you try,

I know how you are so smart yet a little dumb
Maybe you just want to be with someone so you
won't feel numb,

I know how you smirk knowing that you are the
smartest one in the room,
I know how you love shouting the lyrics of your
favourite songs on the top of your lungs,

I know how you are just a cute kid deep down
who just wants to be happy.

Seeing you be you
Seeing you be this angelic
Made me do better too
You are the reason why I did it
I am glad I pushed myself
You are the reason
I understand myself better.

Journey

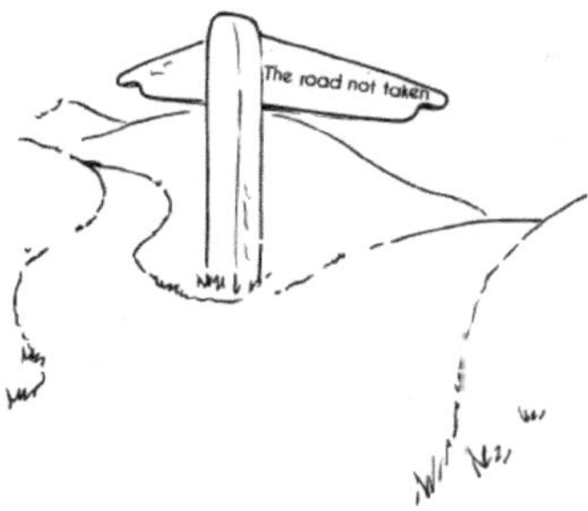

The painful journey
Of going through this healing
Of becoming the person, you are meant to be

Leaving behind the person you are
But you are not exactly who you want to be yet

That in-between
It kills you
You feel clueless
Nameless
Soulless
As if you don't have an identity anymore
All you see is the long weary path ahead of you
You feel uncomfortable and in pain all the time

But you can't give up
You know you can't

You can't go back to who you were
The only way through is to keep moving
forward
And to keep going
And take comfort in knowing that
You are not alone
I don't know about the rest of the world
But you will find me on this path
And we will exchange greetings.

Better

When you get to know yourself better
It scares you
It sure is liberating,
But it scares you because you know now
How easy it is for you to detach from people
How easy it is for you to turn your feelings off
How easy it is for you to choose to be alone
Not that it was always easy
But circumstances made you that way
But now that you are
And now that you know
Does it scare you too?

Great Humbling

Life humbles you
Along you go
And you learn to
Sit alone
At breakfast
For lunches
On dinner tables
And then at night
You learn how to lay all alone
With nothing but your thoughts
Which is a different type of war
It isolates you
To test you
Try not to break under pressure
Because no matter what they say

Your presence will always and always
Be far more powerful
Than your absence
You Matter!!!

Changing Perspectives

Notice how the rooms look larger
When they are empty
And they look smaller
When filled with furniture
That's what loneliness is like
You feel like you are sitting alone
In an empty room
And the only way
To make it smaller
Is to start adding little pieces of furniture
In your room
Day by day
My only advice is
To be picky with it
Try a million little hobbies
Then choose the ones you like
Be as selective as you can be

With the people you let in
And watch them light up your room
Just make sure
You don't leave the room empty
Don't sit alone in the dark

Wisdom

Do you remember the person
Who was there for you
The one who knows about all your struggles
The one who shared the pain
The one who is aware of all your traumas
The one who kept fighting back to make you
win
The one who just didn't give up
Close your eyes
It's you
The one who was there throughout
Without fail
Now tell me
Don't you want this version to think the world of
you
Don't you think this version deserves the world
from you
You deserve it all
All of your love and acceptance

Its time to start putting yourself first
Start loving yourself as deeply as your first love
Start valuing your opinions just as much as you
value the words of loved ones
Because
In the end

It will be you
The one who's going to be there for you
Till the end
It's you.

Time for a change

I think it is time
To change
The plot
Instead of sacrificing the female leads
Try sacrificing the male ones
And witness
The difference in power
The rise of new empires
Basking in glory
As for the old ones
They won't fall
They will transition
You will see them come to light
As they say
The ones capable of creating lives
Lead Differently

The Truth

The Truth is,
No one will ever know
The entire story
Your entire story
No one will know about the time
When it was hard to get out of bed
But you did it anyway
No one will know about the endless tears
And scars on your hands, but you carried on
anyway
No one will be able to relate to the unbearable
pain
That came with the mountain of sadness and
vain
The joy
The grief
And everything in between
Some of these battles
Some of these losses

And
Some of these wins
They are just for you
Just your own
To stay with you
To set you free.

My Soul

As I came face to face
To the little girl
Under my frame
I fell to my knee
There were no more walls
I could see her clearly
Holding on to every bit of strength
To keep going through the storm
Eyes drowned in hopeful tears
Endearing movements full of fear
Stretching her toes
To reach out to me
She whispered
Don't you see
You are the reason
Why I kept going
You are why I kept going
I did it all for you
Now it's your time and I know you will make
me proud
The crown is all yours now
Make sure you keep it shiny and straight
From one queen to the next
It's time for me to rest
For
I shall see you again soon

When the lights will fall
From the heavens
And these merry flowers will bloom
Taking us back
To where we belong
Back to the merry skies
Once and for all.

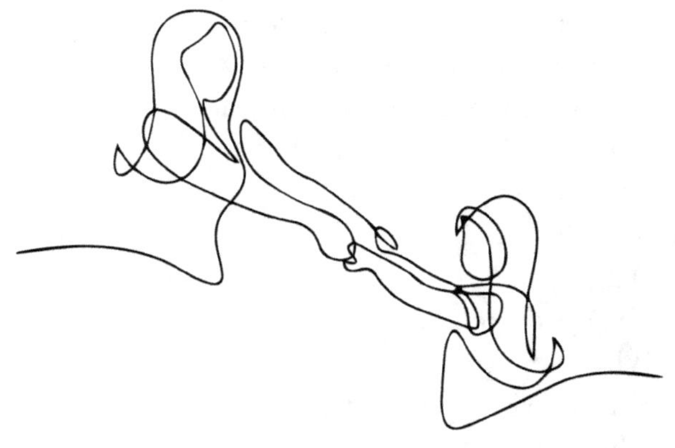

Homesick

I thought I was homesick
For a different place
So, I traveled far
Across the seas
To different skies
But still ended up looking back, feeling lost and
lonely
I thought I was homesick
For a different season
So, I stopped to witness the rebirth of leaves
Thought they might bring me glee
But still ended up looking for fall
I thought I was homesick
For a different time
So, I wandered around at twilight
Wandering these streets with no lights
But still ended up waiting for the crack of dawn
I thought I was homesick
For a person
But still ended up feeling gloomy amidst all my
loved ones and all the merry
All these years
All these thoughts
All these journeys
I thought I was homesick for another entity
Something different

Something holy
Turns out I was homesick for a home
That I left years ago in a hurry
Guess it's time for me to go back home
And take the journey
I have to go back home to me
It's been quite a while
And
I finally realized
I am just homesick for me.

The warrior

If you pulled yourself
Out of a dark space today
If you managed to put
All the shattered pieces
Of your heart back together

If you managed to smile today
In quite a long while
If you got out of bed and
Managed to go out and adore the world

Then believe me
You are it
The ones they talk about in fairytales
Unbreakable soul and iron-clad fists
Heart of a tiger, in battles persist.
If you can put yourself back together
After all the hurt and the damage

All by yourself
Time and again
Then you are built for anything
You are the warrior
A force to be reckoned with.

Little Girl

Walk through the fire
And I will be right by your side
Going up in flames with you

I will burn bridges for you
And help you rebuild them whenever needed

Prepare for battle
Put on the armour
And I will be right next to you
All geared up
Ready to fight the world with you

Speak up
Don't be afraid
Question their norms
And

Change the fate
I will be your voice of reason
And I will absorb all the hate

-A note from the little girl inside who never
stopped fighting back.

Holding up a mirror

So, what do you see
When you look at people around you?
Are you able to take a peek into their souls
Or
Do they act as a reflective mirror of your own
soul?

Do they take you on a journey of your own?

What a funny thing it is
To lose yourself in other people
Only to end up finding yourself.

To my girls

To all my girls
Who are disappointed by this modern world
Do not wait for someone to take you
Through a rabbit hole
And drop you off into a fairytale
Create it for yourself
If you don't like the reality
Escape it
Create a new one for yourself
Be as delusional as you can be
Until and unless
It ends up creating a new reality for you

Women

Women
These magnificent creatures
They take the knife
That was plunged into their hearts
Only to
Turn it into
A makeup accessory for shaping eyebrows
And drawing up winged liners

They are crazy enough to bang on and
Break down the gates of hell
For justice
And yet,
Patient enough to let karma play its role
As their representative

And you ask me
Why am I in awe?

Growing up

Growing up,
I remember
Clenching my fists
Every time I wanted to lash out
Every time I wanted to scream and shout
And just wanted to cry my heart out
Instead, I learned to gulp my anger down
Every now and then
Just clenched my fists
And plastered a poker face
Too afraid to commit any sin
The combat became too frequent
And the walls became too frail
But this time around
When they attacked again
I didn't struggle to lift up the swords

Instead, I clenched my fists and found my
powerhouse of rage again
Now that it has been unlocked
And the games have begun
The only person coming out alive
Is me
And my pain

Hold Yourself

Doesn't your own presence on this earth
Overwhelms you?

Does it fill you up with love and gratitude for
yourself?
Does it make you want to love yourself more?

Looking back at all that you have gone through
Doesn't it light you up?

We got too caught up in the
Black and white
And forget to weigh in the grey

Too busy accusing yourself for all you did
wrong
When was the last time you held yourself close
And thanked yourself

For making it through hell
And for placing you here
In this current moment.

Embracing The Dark

You can feel it.
At times,
That soft soul of yours
Transitioning into something dark
Piece by piece
Bit by bit
Inch by inch
Might not happen consistently
But every now and then
A heart-shattering event might occur
Convincing you to give in to the dark
And soon enough
You will look into the mirror
And find a completely different person standing
in front of you
The question is,
Will you accept yourself?

Or
Spend the better half of your life fighting it
and like the rest of the world
hiding it away.

Pick-Me-Up Girl

Ever since I was a little kid
Whenever good things happened to me
I used to wonder as to why
Why am I being blessed?

And because nobody ever taught me
That I deserved all the good that the universe has
to offer in the first place

I always ended up linking it with an act of
service
Assuming that good only happens to you
When you perform acts of service

So,
I became,
A diligent daughter,

A responsible sister,
A trustworthy friend,
A loyal partner
And
A shoulder to cry on
A book to seek advice from
A tune to soothe the heart

I became the pick-me-up girl.

NATURE'S NOVELTIES

Step into the poetic tapestry of nature and symbolism, where verses unfold like leaves in the breeze, carrying the essence of the earth's beauty and the mysteries of the soul. In this section, each poem is a symbolic exploration, inviting readers to decipher the language of nature's whispers and delve into the profound connections between the tangible and the metaphorical. Embrace the enchantment of the natural world intertwined with the deeper symbolism that unveils the hidden meanings within every leaf, petal, and sunrise.

Moonlike presence

Like the moon
That stays in the sky
It shows up night after night
For you
So that you can talk your heart out
So that you can let the tears fall away
So that you can let the hope in your heart
It shows up consistently
Even when it is not full
It shows up in all of its phases
And on the night of a new moon
You may not be able to see it
But
You still feel its presence all around you

This is what I want to be
To you
Your gateway
To peace
To be your moon
To be a bright presence

Take me

Take me to the world
You slip off to
When you zone out
In the middle of conversations
Before these sunsets
And
After these heartaches
Do you find peace there?
Is it comforting?
Are you all alone?
Can I accompany you?
Do the rainbows have brighter colours there?
Does the sun stay a little longer
And
Does the moon arrive a bit early
Now that they are together in the same sky
Are they finally happy there?

Does the waves kiss the shorelines more gently
Does the rain carry glitters
Do the flowers bloom better?
Are you all alone?
But more importantly
Tell me,
Does it make you happy?
Do you finally feel seen?
Tell me why do you escape?

Chaos

People who grew up in chaos
Like falling asleep with
Trains running in the background
Screaming in the backroom
And crying in the closets
And it is my sincere wish
For all of them
I hope you find your peace
I hope you learn to fall asleep
To soothing rainfall
Instead of the chaotic thunderstorms

Magic shop

Entering a bookshop is just
As enchanting as entering a magic shop
You find rare gems
That help you ease your pain
You find doorways to a new dimension
That helps you escape this tiresome reality
You find voices
That guide you back home to yourself
You find charms
That help you sleep better at night
No matter
What you end up finding
You always walk out of one
With a wide smile
And a heart full of sunshine
A merrier soul
And just a tiny bit happier than before

Angels & Demons

The angels have wings
And so do the demons
The angels have long gowns and crowns
And so do the demons
They both have higher powers
The angels have the Lord
And the demons have the Satan
The angels grant your wishes
And so do the demons
The angels fight your battles for you
And the demons stand right beside you
The only difference is
The bargain
Will you sell your soul for salvation
Or will you settle for a heart and a little pain

Will it be a diamond crown?

With blood and scars
Or
Will it be a golden halo
With the moon and stars

Tell me.
Will you grab the silver melds?
Or
Go straight for the burning pots of gold

Forever?

Fall in love with an artist.
They immortalize you.
They capture the essence of everything that you
do.
They capture the essence of you.
The way you breathe
The way you smile
The way your existence lights up their world
You stay immortalized in their art.
So, tell me, my love.
Will you be my muse?
Would you like to live forever too?

My liberation

Why does love have to come with possession
Why can't it just come with release
Wherein you let go of all the limitations holding
you back
To get to somewhere only you know and only
you can go
Where you lose all your sanity to hold so
strongly
Onto something so fragile
Why does it have to come with an obsession
Why can't it just come with depth
Which pushes you to explore parts of yourself
That has been in hiding for so long
Which encourages you to swim into the deep
ocean residing inside of you
Your love should make you feel like you want to
be better,

Your love should be your strength
Your love should be your motivation
Your love should be your inspiration
And most importantly,
It should be your liberation.

Magic

I know magic is real
When I found myself smiling
Even on the days, my heart was breaking apart,

The sun shined warmly on my face
Showing me all of the glory that exists
In this world
And inside of me
Reminding me of the warmth
That the universe has to offer
And the one that exists within me
Even though the world may seem darker at times

I find peace in remembering that
I will always have the universe with me
Right by my side
The winds are going to take my tears away

The trees are going to protect me
The stars are going to give me hope
The earth is going to keep me grounded
And through it all
I will find myself standing against the storms
Knowing well enough that my soul is strong
Enough to survive on its own
And what a brave little soldier that makes me.

Mosaic Entity

I am a museum
Housing all the people
I have met in this lifetime
In the form of paintings

Some of them are
Contemporary
Some of them are
Abstract
Some of them are
Mere sketches
And
Some of them
Doesn't make a lot of sense
But when you see it
From outside
As a whole
It makes sense,

And
It makes me whole
A complete me
A mosaic entity.

Sacred Place

I hope you find yours
The place you can run back to
When things get bad again
When you feel the burden of this world on your
shoulders again
A sacred place
That one place that welcomes you
Time and again
With open arms
Take the weight off of your shoulders
And tend to your wounds
It can be a person
It can be a lake
It can be a special building

Wherever and whatever it is
I hope you find it
Soon
Your own place
Your sacred place.

Choice

We don't get to choose
If we will lose a person or not
We do however get to choose
If we want to love them or not

For a little as they want to stay
Or
For as long as you want to hold onto them

We won't get to choose how they will leave us
But
We will get to choose how we will make them
feel

Be it as little as a few minutes
Or
As long as a few lifetimes
Your love will always speak

And they will always remember
How you made them feel

ENCHANTED ECHOES

Welcome to the enchanting realm of love and romance, where emotions blossom like petals in the garden of the heart. In this section, each verse is a delicate dance between passion and vulnerability, weaving tales of affection that transcend time and resonate with the timeless echoes of the human soul.

Sparkle

The way your eyes sparkle
When you smile
It lights up my life
And I think that is what's keeping me alive,

The way you laugh
Brings me back to life and
These giggles fill up my life
And make me smile,

The way you make me laugh
Even when we are miles apart
Is like a warm blanket to my heart.

Declaration

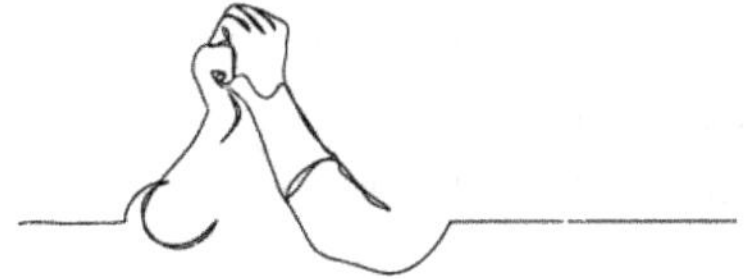

Maybe this is it
My declaration of love for you
I am willing to let you go
To let you find your happiness elsewhere
This is how I am choosing to tell you
Just how much I love you

My love doesn't have limits
It is not traditional
It is not about owning
Wherever you are in this world
My thoughts will always echo your name
Wishing you all my love
And happiness
Just the same,
I will always keep your name in my prayers.

He is it

He is it
He is the in-between
He is all my colors
In between black and white
He is all my emotions
In between crisis and ecstasy
He is all these moments
In between life and death
His is the voice I will follow through the dark
He is not just a part of me
I am him
And
He is me

Overdose

Every now and then
I find myself overdosing
In your thoughts
And
I find myself overindulging
In your praises
But strangely
Those are also the days
When I fall a little more in love with myself
And I don't keep the world at bay
When I stare a little bit longer at my scars in the
mirror
And appreciate them more instead of just
running away

Higher than the sky

Don't you get it?
It's you
It has always been you.
The one I look for
In crowded rooms
And
Empty hallways
The one I always come back to
After traveling the world
The one I want to annoy at 3 a.m.
And
Make love to at 6 p.m.
The one I come to feel at home
After spending the entire day with loved ones
The one I want to sip coffee with first thing in
the morning
The one I want to trade secrets with

The one I can share my darkness with
If you are ever in doubt,
Remember
You are it.
My penny tosses in the wishing well
My Christmas miracle
My New Year's wish
My Twinflame

Talismans

Carry them with you
Little pieces of love
Or souvenirs as I like to call them
So that they can give you strength
From time to time
Carry your mother's jewelry with you
Wear them on days when you want to be
More gentle and kinder to the world
And to yourself
Wear your father's shirts on days
You want to get things done
And need a dose of strength
Wear your brothers' sneakers on days
You want to be more friendly and outgoing
And want to go places
Wear your sisters' hair clips and glittery glosses
On days you want to go back to being a kid
again
And feel that spark from within
Wear your loved one's jacket on days
You want to feel comforted
And want the universe to greet you with a
friendly face again
Carry them with you
All the time
Like talismans

Let them give you strength
Carry love with you
Wherever you go.

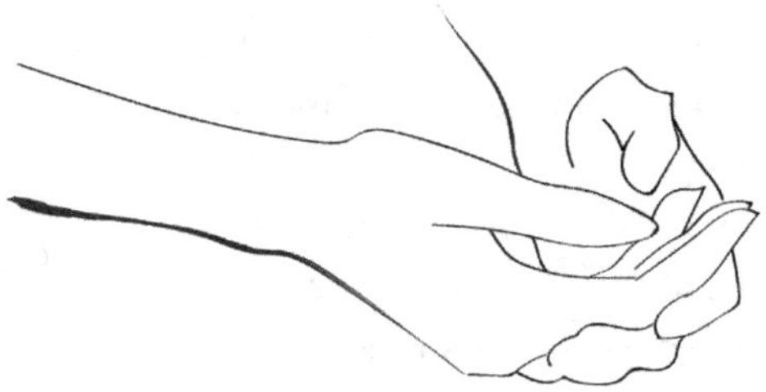

Before & After

Before I met you
I just wanted to be understood
To tell people
Tiny little details
All about me
To make them aware of the what and whatnots
So that they will know
How to love me even deeply
But now
I just want to understand you
Jot down the tiny little details
remember the what and whatnots
and find out at least a thousand ways to please
you
and to love you so dearly
just like you deserve
and then

maybe then
I will be free
I will be shown the reason for my existence
For my being.

Free

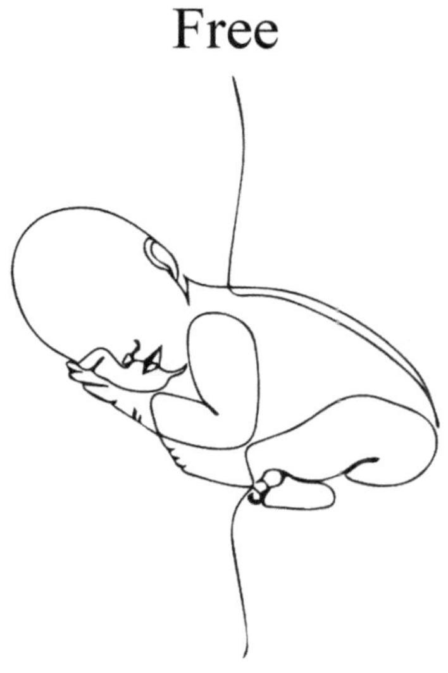

I want to love you like I am not afraid to lose
you
Whether you stay or you go
I will walk forever with you
Like a mother's prayer
And a fallen wish
Like a father's charm
And a twilight's kiss

If I was born
To die
Let me die
All consumed in your beauty
Set me free

Of all cages
Of all fears
Just let me be

If I was born
To die
Let me die
In your love
Let me be.

Power of love

I find it beautiful how we all read the same
poems
Same stories
Same lyrics
And end up thinking of different people
For some of you that person is sitting right next
to you
For some of us they are sitting continents apart
But the way we all feel is the same
The feeling of joy we feel when we come across
a romantic line
Or the way our heart skips a beat when they are
about to hold our hands

The way tears roll down our cheeks when they
are torn apart
The unexplainable power that a love poem holds
By making a million people feel the same
emotions
Has to be proof that
Love is the answer
It is what we fight for
It is what we stand for
It is what unites us
And
In the end, it is what we die for.

Destin

Pick up the markers
And leave a message for me
On the lamppost down the 13th street

I will walk past it again
On a cozy day on the 9th of February
In this lifetime
Or maybe in another infinity

I will see the red link
And know deep in my heart
We will find each other again
Because darling
You and I
Are meant to be!
Throughout all of our infinities.

Cruel Twist

And if by some cruel twist of events
I am not able to understand you
Through words
I promise you that
I will cry with you
I will laugh with you
I will scream with you
And
I will sit in silence with you
Till the day
I am finally able to understand you
I will do.

Your choice

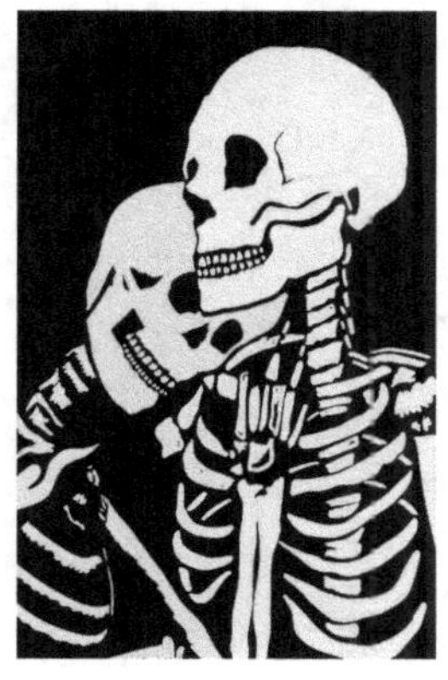

You choose this time
What you want to be
If you want to be a hero
I will gladly ask you to sacrifice me to save the
world
If you want to be a villain
I will quietly let you sacrifice the world to save
me
All the cards are on the table
And I am all in
You choose this time around
And in the end
I will still love you the same

Moments

Every time I look at you
All I want to do is steal more moments with you
And when you look at me
Time starts moving differently
Hours turn into minutes
And minutes into seconds

Every time our eyes meet
Different shades of brown are sprinkled across
the room
This love of mine makes me want to turn into a
poet
Just so I can say a million things to you
All I really want to do
Is run across the room to fall into you

Just to look deeply into your eyes and tell you
how much I missed you
All this time
How patiently I have been waiting for you
But every time I see you
I feel like I am back to sixteen
And I can barely express anything to you

Grown up enough

Now that I am grown up enough
To know what it all means
How deep these bonds run
How valuable promises are
How strong love can be
And
How nearly devastating heartbreaks are
I
With all my awareness
And with my all
Give my heart to you
For the rest of my life
I am giving you the power
To love me
Or
To destroy me
To the core
It is yours

Off the edge

I have always been cautious around people
However,
It is very easy for me to lose myself in the
universe
Into the nature
I can lose myself in the air
I flow with it, wherever it goes
I can lose myself in the clouds
I float with them, however far they travel
I can lose myself in the ocean
I swim with it, at whatever pace it wants me to
I can lose myself in the fire
I burn with it, no matter how fiery it gets
I can immerse myself completely
I like how it feels
The feeling of being safe on the edge
The almost
Of existence
And

Of extinction
I can lose myself in things
But ever since I have met you
I have been terrified
Of how willing I am to fall right off the edge
Just to land right next to you
So that I can lose myself in you

A letter

A letter to my love's dear ones
From the bottom of my heart
I want to thank you all.
For being by my lover's side
Throughout the years
Through all his struggles
Through the pain
Through the losses and the gains
Thank you for making his days brighter.
By adding more light to his victories
Thank you for sheltering him from harm.
By protecting him with love from within
Thank you for crying with him.
Thank you for picking him up.
Thank you for laughing with him.

Thank you for being such a constant presence in
his life.
Thank you for the encouragement and the
motivation.
To be the individual he is today
Thank you for shaping him into the man
That I love so dearly today.
Thank you.

Moons Ago

I loved you once
Many moons ago
And since then
No one came close,
I spend all this time wandering,
Why the only eyes I want to see,
Every morning and every night are yours,

Why the only hand I want to hold,
Throughout all the seasons are yours,

Why the only voice I want to listen to,
On loop in this lifetime is yours,

Why the only pair of arms I want to run back
To escape this strange world is yours,

It is because
You are my home away from home
It all starts and ends with you
Because of your existence
I am now whole.

What Love Is?

I think
That is what love is
To allow people to be themselves
Completely,
Without any judgements
And still love them
Throughout the process
Of them becoming their most authentic selves
And instead of just waiting
For them on the other side
You choose to walk this path
With them
That's what love is
To see your person blossom
And what a privilege it is
To take this journey side by side
With them

The Universe

Two trillion galaxies,
Within them
There is "our Milky Way"

100 billion stars
Within them
There is "our Solar System"

8 planets
Within them
There is "our Earth"

7 continents
7.888 billion people
10 eras
And
You and I exist in the same timeline
Somewhere up there

Must be really happy with me
For allowing me to exist at the same time as you.

All these numbers
All these figures
And then,
There is you and me
Watching the moon every night
Seeing her transition through its beautiful phases
I am grateful.

One

Watch me crumble
As our eyes meet
Watch me burn
As our bodies intertwine
Watch me go insane
As our heartbeats synchronize
Watch me melt
As our souls fuse together

We were never two different atoms
We were one
Complete halves of a circle
Complete loops of an infinity
Watch me fall apart
As we become one again

Completion

If we are what we love
Then I am you
I love you
As far as these grounds stretch
As rich as the blue in the skies
As deep as the oceans run
Believe me hon
I love you
As I do
I am you
we are one
&
I am complete

www.ingramcontent.com/pod-product-compliance
Lightning Source LLC
La Vergne TN
LVHW011020200726
843509LV00011B/1168